How To Start Your Own Highly Profitable Work From Home Business...

In Your Spare Time!

By

Bill Knight

(Author, Direct Response Copywriter, Online Entrepreneur)

Anglox Publications

Published in the UK 2017 by Anglox Publications

Contents

Contents continued

ISBN-13:
978-1546369837

ISBN-10:
154636983X

Chapter 1

Introduction

Be your own boss... work the hours that best suit you... no staff... virtually no overheads... no face to face selling... take time off when you want... create your own products... 100% profits...

UNLIMITED EARNINGS!

Who wouldn't want to be their own boss and work for themselves... from the comfort of their home?

For some people, the very thought of starting a new business venture may seem a little daunting but that's usually because they think it's too difficult or there's just too much involved.

In this guide you're going discover the exact opposite is true. In fact I'm sure many people would jump at the opportunity of starting a profitable home-based business if they only knew how really simple it actually is.

Let's first look at the whole concept of being in business...

It simply means that you will be working for yourself and you can do this either full-time or part-time. There are advantages to both options as you will learn a bit later.

As many people have come to realise, working for yourself is very satisfying and the financial rewards can make it all worthwhile. That said, there may be times when the self-employed person wishes they had the security of a steady job and a regular guaranteed income.

Working for yourself means you have to ensure you have enough money to cover periods when you might be unable to work due to sickness. There might also be times when work can drop off and leave you wondering where your next meal is coming from.

In this guide we explore why working for yourself in the right kind of business can eliminate or at least minimise any such problems. If your business is set up the right way then you will have little to do other than market your products, which is where people in business really make their money.

In the following pages you'll learn what you need to do by way of preparation. What you need to do by UK law, and what you need to do to create a near perfect hands-off type of business.

Some very important factors you should realise are... you do not need any previous business experience... you don't need any business premises... you don't need any staff... and you don't really need any stock.

In fact, done the right way, a successful work at home business can be operated single-handedly from the comfort of your own home and with virtually no overheads and out-goings whatsoever!

Other factors worthy of consideration are financial investment. The least money you need to start up and succeed the better. Then there is the amount of time you might need to devote to setting up your business.

A business is not going to be much fun if you have to spend every waking hour working in it. That's why this guide has been created to help you avoid any pitfalls and ensure your business is both enjoyable and profitable.

Once set up properly, you will discover that it's much more rewarding, in many ways, to work ON your business instead of IN your business.

The purpose of this guide or beginner's course as it is probably best described, it to help generate ideas and inspire you to get started. Many people have said they have thought about working for themselves at some point but then never taken action to make it happen.

A business can offer you a way to financial freedom, which is something you are very unlikely to find if you work all your life for someone else. Why work just to make someone else rich?

There is no one type of business that will make you rich... any business can! You just have to have the commitment and resilience and determination to make it work. There is however, in my opinion, a type of business that can make you very rich, very quickly...

What is the best type of home-based business?

Information Publishing!

Books, reports, guides, tutorials, manuals and DVDs all have a part to play in successful information publishing, so I make no apologies for being a little biased towards these products.

Now, let's go explore the possibilities...

Getting Prepared

Failing to prepare is preparing to fail. Every business starts with a plan, regardless of what type of business it is, or products or services that are to be offered.

However, with a small 'work at home' type of business, there is much less planning to do than if you were going to start a manufacturing business for example.

As this guide is only concerned with the home-based business type, where one person or perhaps a partnership are involved, I will refer only to what is needed in setting up this type of business.

First there are some essentials you will need and they include a computer. This can be a desktop PC or a laptop, with preferably a Windows operating system (Windows 7, 8 or above), and access to the internet. You will also need a word processing program and a spreadsheet program.

These software programs can be Microsoft Word and Microsoft Excel, although the Microsoft Works suite will do just as well.

You will need to be able to transfer your files onto a CD or print out all your invoices, so that you have a hard copy of all your records and business transactions. So, a printer and a CD writer, the latter being available on most computers, are also requirements.

Now, there is one piece of equipment, which I highly recommend you do have and that's a good video camcorder. It will pay for itself in next to no time.

The next thing you want to consider is where you are going to work from. A spare room is ideal but any quiet area, where you can work undisturbed will do. The proverbial "Kitchen Table" has been an adequate resource for many a new start-up.

4

Even the garage has been used successfully to start a small business... in fact that's how the world famous Amazon Company began its life.

Now, every business needs a name. This is a trading name, by which you will be known, and of which you will notify HMRC.

Many individuals use their own name or their initials as a business name. For example, if your name is John Paul Maxwell, then your business name could be JPM followed by whatever relates to the business you will be in.

In the case of information products, which I highly recommend, and which are highly profitable, your business name could become, JPM Publishing or JPM Distribution.

You'll learn more about information products and other products as you progress through this guide.

So, what's in a name?

Many companies and indeed some individuals will select a business name that can be easily remembered. For marketing and branding purposes these memorable names can become embedded in our daily lives.

Names such as Coca Cola, Virgin, Nike and Amazon are instantly recognisable because they have become synonymous with the products or services they represent.

A well-known business name can become a brand and branding also helps to build trust and loyalty. However, branding may be something you will want to consider once your business has become well established, so no need to concern yourself with branding at this stage.

One thing to bear in mind when deciding on a trading name is whether you will at some point in the future need a website. Virtually every type of business needs a web presence so I would highly recommend this.

The reason I mention this is because you might want to consider using your trading name as a domain name also. And that's if you can get it. For example, let's say you decided on a trading name like Maxwell Publishing. You might also want to register a domain name which includes this: maxwellpublishing.co.uk

It is not essential to have the same domain name as your trading name but it can keep everything tidy in respect of marketing.

It's best to read through this complete guide before deciding on exactly what to produce or sell, and then you can decide on a relevant trading and domain names for your business.

As for advertising your business, the general idea for a start-up is to generate enough income from your business in the initial stages, to pay for any future advertising overheads.

When everything else is in place, the last part of the preparation work is to notify HMRC that you will be starting self-employment. Again this can be on a part-time basis or full-time.

I should point out here that it is perfectly legal to start up a business even if you have a full-time job working for someone else.

I'll cover all of these points in more detail in a forthcoming chapter. I just want you to see exactly what you need to do before your business is up and running.

So, once you have notified HMRC, then you're good to go.

Now, one of the reasons why some people are put off starting their own business is because they think you have to register your business with Companies House, and you have to register for VAT.

You don't have to do either and I recommend you don't, certainly not at the initial stage.

If you form a company and register that company then you have to appoint directors, and you will need an accountant. This means you'll be getting involved in things that make running a business a real pain in the neck... and unnecessarily expensive

Working as a sole trader you don't have to do this so why do it?

And do you really want to become an unpaid tax collector? Accounting for VAT means more work for you so why do it when you don't have to?

If your business turnover looks like it's going to exceed £83,000 (at time of writing) then you will have to register, but until it does don't worry about it. My advice is to stay under the VAT threshold and save yourself a lot of grief.

So let's go through the preparation checklist:

1. Computer with internet access and word processing and spreadsheet software installed.

2. Printer and CD writer, copier paper and blank CDs for keeping copies of all transactions.

3. A telephone. Obvious I know but just to mention here that a mobile phone will do.

4. A cheap but capable camcorder. You can pick one up on ebay for under £50.

5. Somewhere to work. Preferably a spare room, although a quiet area of any room will do.

6. After you have decided on what you are going to sell, decide on a business trading name and notify HMRC.

7. Register your website domain names.

Registering Your Business

Let's now look at some of the preparation steps in more detail, and we'll start with registering your business with HMRC.

HMRC don't really consider this action as 'registering a business', it's more like registering as a sole trader or to become self-employed.

It doesn't matter what they want to call it, you still have to do this part as it is a legal requirement. However, there's nothing to it as you'll see.

First, go to this HMRC webpage:
https://www.gov.uk/working-for-yourself/what-you-need-to-do - and read the guidance notes.

After you have read the information go to this link: https://www.gov.uk/new-business-register-for-tax - do this even if you are starting out on a part-time basis.

The main reason why you must do this because you will have to complete an online Self-Assessment for tax and NI contributions.

Don't worry, it's very easy to do and there are some real financial benefits to being both employed and self-employed as I'll explain a little later.

When you're ready, click the big green 'Start Now' button on the HMRC registration page to get the ball rolling, and stay on the right side of the law.

Keeping Records

Okay, that's all the legal stuff done, except remember! You MUST keep records of all business transactions. I'll now explain the best way to do all that necessary record keeping.

First, just get yourself a simple file folder for any paper invoices, so that you have everything in one place. The worst thing you can do with running any type of business, is to be unorganised when it comes to keeping all your paperwork together. This little regular task can save you hours when it comes to the end of your financial year.

Although your trading period is the date, at which you will have been trading for a full year. I recommend that whatever date you start your business, you aim to get your accounting period in line with the financial year. This runs from April 6th to April 5th in the following year. This will make life so much easier when it comes to working out your tax liabilities for the year.

So for example, if you start a business on say November 25th, then you should aim to keep records for the period November 25th to April 5th, and then start again from April 6th up to April 5th in the following year. These dates will become your accounting period.

Okay, so a simple folder for paper invoices... and now how to set up a spreadsheet for your other records.

The best program to use for this is MS Excel, which you will probably already have on your computer. Open up the program and save the page as Accounts or Records followed by the year. For example, Accounts-2017.

Then you need to create some headers for the columns you will need. You can be as inclusive as you want here but I'm only going to cover the basic set up because this is the minimum you will need.

In the first row, type the same heading as you gave the page. Then in column no.1, type 'Name' Column no.2, type 'Address', column no.3 type 'Postcode' and then in column no.4, type 'Email'. These will be records of your customers.

You can of course add as much information as you want but this is probably the minimum. I should mention, you don't have to do this by law, this exercise is for your own benefit.

And you might not have to do all of this or any at all depending on the type of business you set up.

Now, at the bottom left of the MS Excel spreadsheet, click on the plus symbol and add another page.

Next, put some column headers starting with, 'Accounts 2017/18' or whatever accounting period / year the spreadsheet relates to. Then in the next column put the header, 'Money Banked' or something similar. Then in the left-hand column below the headings put the title 'Income' followed by the 12 months.

On this spreadsheet you will keep records of all your income month by month. Make sure you cross check with your bank statements to ensure the figures are correct.

I recommend you keep all your records up to date on a monthly basis. You can of course add more information about the products you have sold if you wish but this is the minimum number of records needed here.

Okay... next, click on the plus button again, situated at the bottom left-hand side of the page and open up another new page. Here is where you will keep records of all your business transactions.

You will need a number of headings on this sheet so that you can see at a glance your outgoings and overheads.

Include things like phone, heating & lighting, postage, software, domains & hosting, equipment & repairs, advertising, outsource fees, and anything else that will need to spend money on during the course of running your business.

You will be able to claim a tax allowance for most of these expenses, and it's these allowances, which will offset all your tax liabilities.

Once you have created this spreadsheet with the relevant column headings, you can then add any others as you go, should they become necessary.

On the subject of tax allowances, you can claim allowances for using your home, or part of it, as an office. You can also claim for lighting and heating, use of telephone and internet. However, be realistic about the amounts you claim. If you are only using a corner of a room then you should be looking to claim less than if you have dedicated a whole room to operating your business.

For further guidance on allowances check out this web page: https://www.gov.uk/expenses-if-youre-self-employed/overview

On top of these allowances your main allowance will be your tax free allowance. At the time of writing this is £10,000, which means your first £10,000 of profits is tax free.

Outsourcing

So, hopefully you will now be up to speed about what you need to do to set up and register your own business, and as you can see there's nothing too difficult about it. However, if you don't want to bother doing any of the record keeping tasks, you can always outsource this work to an accounts firm or a bookkeeper.

You'll find many bookkeepers online if you search on Google.

It's not uncommon for people in business to outsource many of the mundane day to day tasks or even hire a local freelancer to do the work. If you're budget will stretch to this and you really don't want to do it yourself then go ahead and hire someone.

Now, there are certain aspects of your information publishing business, which you will most likely have to outsource. I'm talking about the duplication of your information products and fulfilment of your orders. It's unlikely you will have the necessary duplication equipment at home and your products do have to be professionally copied, including the artwork.

These days there are companies that will do just about everything for you, from taking the order, DVD duplication, packaging, invoicing and postage. This leaves you free to concentrate on your marketing, which is less hands-on but much more rewarding.

If you would prefer to have more control over the order processing, I'll cover that option in just a moment.

Now, for full processing you will need to check out the companies that are available to you. I can't recommend any one company myself because much will depend on things like your budget and volume of orders.

However, I can suggest you contact a few and discuss your requirements with them. Some of them are happy to bill you for their services, whilst others might insist they collect the full payments from your customers and then pass on the remaining profits, after all fees have been deducted.

You will need to decide which company is going to be best for your operation.

Here are some links to fulfilment companies that you could try:

http://www.mediaplant.co.uk/dvd-fulfilment/

http://www.efulfillmentservice.com/cd-dvd-media/

http://www.tcsoho.tv/services/dvd-cd-duplication-and-replication-packing-and-fulfilment/

http://www.cd-fulfillment.com/

http://www.know-solutions.com/cd-dvd-bluray-fulfilment-and-distribution.php

http://www.corefulfilment.com

As you can see there are quite a few and if you searched Google for 'Fulfilment Company' you'll find a heck of a lot more.

Basically all you would need to do is send the fulfilment company your master DVDs and some images for the covers and they will take care of the rest.

In terms of processing orders they may have their own preferred way of dealing with this so you will need to find out more information in advance.

Now, for those on a tight budget and who are a little savvy at using the Internet, you can use a different type of company for your order processing.

The company is called Kunaki and their website is: www.kunaki.com

Now this company offers professional duplication and order processing at some very affordable prices, however there is a catch or I should say a series of catches...

They are based in the USA and can take 7-10 days to get the order to your customer.

You have to upload your DVD masters, your own artwork, photos etc and design the DVD covers.

The upside is, this is very easy to do and very rewarding because you have complete control of the design of your own products.

The finished product is very professional complete with bar code and cellophane wrapped, and the best way to get around the shipping time is to order small batches (5 or 10) to be delivered to your address and send them out from there.

If you decide to go for ordering small batches then beware the customs and excise charges. Just order about 10 DVDs at a time and you should be okay.

The DVDs cost around $1 each plus P&P, so there's big profits to be had by doing it this way.

I'll quickly go over what you need to do should you decide on this very low cost option...

First you open an account and then you will use their software to upload your master DVD.

Once uploaded you can then design the DVD case cover, which will be similar to the printed disc image. You can add a title, sub title and copyright information and other information if appropriate.

Once these masters have been designed you can then simply order as you wish.

You can also design a web page to sell your DVDs from, which is great for those on a limited budget, as there is no charge for this.

There are many advantages to using Kunaki, if you are just starting out and you have some experience of working on the Internet and using software programs.

Whether you choose this option or the fulfilment option, your business is just a step away from making some real money.

Summary

By now you should have realised that the main money making type of business I'm steering you towards is Information Publishing and the DVD will be the main vehicle for your products.

Information publishing has been responsible for creating literally hundreds of millionaires over the years.

First it was information sold by Direct Mail that made people very rich, now it's the same type of information but now it's sold over the Internet and sent out as DVD products.

You can of course start up any type of business and we will take a look at some of the many options later in this guide. However, in my experience, Information Publishing, which includes 'How To' videos, is by far the most lucrative.

Before you move forward from this 'Getting Started' stage into full production and marketing let's just check that you have done everything you need to do this far...

1. Make sure you have everything you need in place and ready to go. It's important to be well prepared before you start and it will make life easier as you progress.

2. Ensure you have registered with HMRC and you are trading legally. Remember, you can start part-time and still work at your regular job until you are earning enough to go full-time.

Or, just keep the business as a part-time operation. It's up to you but even if you only operate your business part-time you can still claim the taxable allowances (except personal allowance), which means you will be paying less tax all round.

3. Make sure you keep records of everything. That includes all out-goings and income. You cannot claim expenses if you don't have the paperwork to match, and the last thing you will want is the tax man on your case.

4. Decide on which outsourcing option would suit you best. You won't know this right now, but by the time you have read this complete guide you will have a good idea about what you can do yourself and what you will need others to do for you.

5. Finally, Enjoy what you are doing. If you're making money then it's always easy to enjoy your business but even if business is slow, don't give up because you could just be one very tiny step away from huge success.

In this next chapter, you'll learn about how to create your very own products to sell. This is about creating products that could make you a ton of money.

Chapter 2

Introduction

For many years product marketers both offline and online have been quietly making small fortunes from selling easy to acquire information.

Information products have accounted for many millions of pounds in sales because people are simply willing to pay good money to find out how to do things.

The most common information product is the business opportunity type, where a 'How To' guide is written and then sold for silly prices. Silly prices they may be, but people want them and will pay real and serious money for them.

Now here's an example, let's say you have an idea about how to make money from sports betting. You have devised a system that proves to pay you a 20% profit on every bet.

So you write a manual or guide about how you do it and throw in a few screen shots and perhaps an image of your bank balance and then you get the manual printed.

Next, you rent a mailing list from a reputable list broker and you send out a sales letter to this list about your new money-making idea and offer to sell them the manual.

You want £97 for your manual and you tell your prospects they could make this money back within just a few days.

You send out 10,000 sales letters to the list and you get a 3% response.

Now let's do the maths...

10,000 x 3% = 300 sales @ £97 = £29,100

Less of course your expenses, i.e., copywriting of sales letter, postage, printing and stationery.

Let's look at the expenses to see how much actual profit this exercise would make.

Copywriting £400

Printing of letters and manual £1,150

Postage of sales letters and manual £5,950

Other expenses (incidental) £300

That's a total of £7,800 for expenses = Over £21,000 pure profit!

Worth doing?

Of course and this is still being done today only on a much smaller scale than it was say 20-30 years ago. A UK company called Streetwise Publications is just one such company, which handles all the sales, marketing, promotional and distribution of information products, which are created by individual entrepreneurs.

If you're good at writing then there's still plenty of mileage in this type of product. However, the easier and much cheaper DVD option is still hands down the winner when it comes to perceived value of a product and it has the edge.

It's much easier for people to learn about something if they can see it being demonstrated, rather than reading about it.

Product Creation

So, do you want to make at least £20K profit from each mail campaign?

What about £20K - £30K profit from every DVD information product?

It's not beyond anyone's ability to repeat this process at least once a month and in fact the profits can be much, much higher if you combine a direct mail campaign with an online campaign.

So, we've established that selling information products through mail order is worth doing and a website will only increase your chances of making even more money but what product is going to make the most money?

The answer is a unique product that cannot be bought anywhere else...

That means you will have to create it from scratch, but as I have already indicated, an information product is not too difficult to create. You only have to put in the time and effort.

Information sells like hot cakes all over the world. Every day someone somewhere is buying an information product about something. It will probably always be that way so it's an opportunity that cannot be ignored.

Now, when you think about it there is the possibility of creating an information product about absolutely anything. However, the best ones will be for the biggest markets.

Some of the biggest markets are health and fitness related, beauty and glamour and personal improvement. Then some of the most popular hobbies in the UK are knitting, fishing, reading, gardening, music, travel and golf.

In fact the list is endless when you consider all the individual sports and activities. So there are boundless opportunities to create products that someone, somewhere will be more than willing to buy.

All you have to do is come up with some ideas about how people can do their hobby better or enjoy their interest more or learn something new that they can benefit from.

So, now we know there is a limitless supply of subjects, on which to create a unique information product, how do we get started?

Well, before we get into that part of the course, I just want to mention that an information product can be a written book or manual, a video or an audio file.

I suggest you pay special attention to the ideas in this manual with a view to creating videos for sale.

Then, if you haven't already... go and check out this website: www.kunaki.com - If you're on a low budget this could be your way into making some serious money.

Information Products

Do you have any special interests?

Are you particularly good at something?

Do you know how to fix things or make things?

You might not realise it but you probably have a goldmine of information stored in your head, and someone, somewhere will actually pay you for it. So that's where you should probably start on your quest for subject matter.

Start by listing all the things you are good at and knowledgeable about, and then put them in order of importance... to you! That's right! The more important they are to you, the more likely you are to have a lot of knowledge about them.

So, once you've gone through this exercise, the next thing to do is start writing or, in the case of video start filming.

It's okay to do research on the Internet to fill in gaps or substantiate the information. Everyone does this.

I know you might be thinking... well anyone can just search the internet to find the information I want to write about so what's the point?

Well, the point is, people are generally lazy. If they can get all the information they need from one convenient source, chances are they will pay for it, so don't be put off.

If you decide to write an information product, like a manual, you may need to add screenshots, images or photos to the manual to better explain the subject, so be prepared to do this. Smartphones have pretty good cameras these days and there's plenty of free software products to help you, so there's no excuse.

Now, if after racking your brains you cannot for the life of you come up with anything of interest, which might inspire someone to buy from you then here's what to do...

Ask someone else!

You must know someone who is good at or knowledgeable about something. A friend? Relative? Retired teacher, accountant, lawyer, doctor, tax advisor etc?

A car mechanic... a landscape gardener... upholsterer... builder... and the list could go on and on.

Once you've identified a likely source, ask if you can interview them and offer to pay them or buy them a beer or lunch or something in return for their time.

Then once you have the interview recorded, you can get the recording transcribed and there you have it... your unique information product.

Many successful products have come about by this method so it's already been tried and tested... and proven.

A 50-60 page manual on a specialist subject will sell for between £37 and £97 depending on how complex the subject is. For example, a 60 page manual about pruning fruit trees might sell for £37, whilst a 40 page guide about making money from spread betting could easily sell for £97.

It's all about perceived value.

If you look at it this way...

Someone needs a new fence at the bottom of their garden. They buy all the panels and posts but need someone to erect it for them. Not because they're too weak to do it themselves, but because they don't know how.

So, they contact a fence erecter who quotes them £200 plus VAT for the work. A manual about how to easily erect a panel fence could sell for £37, so it's very tempting for the homeowner to buy the manual and save a bundle of cash, by simply doing it themselves.

Here's another example...

Someone has an old BMW 3 series car and it needs a new radiator fitting. The garage quotes £195 plus VAT for supplying and fitting the radiator. Your manual is entitled, "How To Easily And Cheaply Fit A New Radiator Into A BMW 3 Series".

In the manual you tell the reader where to buy a replacement radiator for £45, and the manual is full of step-by-step images showing every stage of the removal and fitting process. Your manual sells for £67. That's a saving of around £189 for the DIY car enthusiast... for about an hour's work.

That's great... if you like writing but what if you don't? Well, you simply get someone else to transcribe the audio recording for you. Go and look at www.upwork.com and www.freelancer.com – On these websites, you could get the work done for a few dollars!

Now, instead of a manual you could have a video made showing every stage of the process, which is very often much easier for the customer to follow. The video could still be sold at the same price or more.

To create a video like this, get in touch with a few local garages and ask them to let you know when they are going to be doing some work that you can film.

They could become the star of your video plus you can recompense them for their time, and still have a very profitable and unique product.

Just think about all the different jobs and tasks you could apply this format to...

Bricklaying... turf laying... window fitting... electrical work... PC repairs... manicures... dog grooming... plumbing... decorating... and so on.

Remember! Once you create a video it becomes your property. You own all the rights to it and you can duplicate it over and over and sell the DVD products as your own.

You can charge whatever price you want and keep all of the profits for yourself.

Now I'm going to let you into a little secret.

In fact this secret has accounted for many millions of pounds in profits. I know of one man who has made over £30 million and another who has made at least £20 million from doing this...

Selling licenses to your own products.

Basically, you create DVD information products and you allow others to sell them or copy them and sell them under licence. It's called a reseller licence.

You create the licence, give them a copy of a master DVD product and charge them anything from £500 to £1,000 per product license. They can then rebrand the product as their own.

This is how you get seriously rich!

Software Products

Some fortunes have been made online by people who have created software products. I mean, many millions of pounds can be made if you can come up with an idea that will save people time and money.

Recently there has been an upsurge in the creation of apps (applications) because smartphones are great at running them, and simply because so many people have smartphones. The apps are relatively cheap to create and generally sell for under £2, but you can still make tons of money due to the sheer volume of sales.

You only have to have an app or software program built once and it can go on providing you with an income for many years.

The Wordpress blogging platform is another fine example because anyone who can code can create a 'plugin' for Wordpress and sell this to the many millions of people who have Wordpress websites.

Now, don't worry if you're not the technical type because you only have to come up with an idea. There are tens of thousands of programmers and coders out there who will build your app or software product for you for a very reasonable price.

To find them go to www.freelancer.com and place a job ad. You'll get dozens of applicants who will bid against each other to do the job for you... for just a few quid.

Software sells extremely well on the Internet, especially if it is something that will save people time and money or can make them money. For example, a program that can help you make videos on your computer can sell for $97 and you can upsell to your customers with add-ons and developer licenses etc.

One good product can set you up for life.

The best way to find out what people need and are willing to pay for is to sign up to as many forums as possible. That way you can follow the threads of the many topics and see what people are talking about. Most people use forums to find information that will help them in their online business or with their hobbies or interests.

This is an absolute goldmine of information in itself because many questions get answered and these same questions keep getting asked over and over.

All you have to do is document them and you have a product to sell.

Software that can create things like virtual book covers, or e-covers as they are known, have made lots of cash for their creators. The same goes for banner making software and logo making software.

If you think along the lines of what people need to promote their products and services online, then you can come up with some good ideas about software that can help them.

Just take your idea to a developer and agree a price for the work. Then get busy marketing your new software product to the masses.

Let's look at a possible scenario...

Countless online business people are in need of a product that will automatically update their Facebook page. So you go to a developer and agree to get this software created. The developer wants $500 and agrees to hand over all rights to you when the job is complete.

The software gets created and you set up a website to market the product plus you create your own Facebook page to help promote the products also.

The software is going to save numerous hours of manually updating these Facebook pages so people can instantly see the advantage and benefits.

So, you decide this is a worthy piece of kit and you already know there is a massive market for it, so you sell it at $197 per download. An instant download means no shipping and handling. Not only have you created an in-demand product but the whole business can be put on auto-pilot, leaving you free to enjoy the money.

Now what about the money?

This is a serious product with a market to match so realistically you could sell over a million downloads before someone else jumps in and copies it. By that time you won't be too worried because you will have already made in excess of $190 million from just one product.

It's what dreams are made of but if you don't dream to live, you'll never live the dream.

There are many online success stories like this and there's many more to come, especially as the Internet grows and diversifies. The needs become more...

Get your thinking cap on... or at least do some research.

The funny thing about getting really excited about creating products from your own ideas is... the more you start thinking about them, the more ideas you get...

Try it!

Membership Websites

Another great way to make good money online... on a regular basis, is a membership website.

The idea behind a membership site is you become an expert in your field and you drip feed your members vital snippets of information.

For example, if you were into trading Forex, you might have some insider information that you can email out to your members at a minute's notice, or you might have a tipping service for horse racing or sports betting.

Your members pay a monthly fee to stay in the loop and you keep them happy by continually providing them with valuable information. It's a simple concept and can work well for a whole host of subjects, interests and genres.

However, the emphasis is on providing 'valuable information'. That's what the members are willing to pay for.

Here are a few other examples...

Online courses.

Your members pay a monthly fee to access learning material, and that really can be on any subject. Think about that for a minute.

Also, providing premium website content, such as fresh articles is another idea.

Learn to play a musical instrument, such as guitar or saxophone or piano. If you can play an instrument then there are certainly others who will pay you to teach them. All you have to do is create lessons, video yourself and post them into your membership site for all to see.

Dating websites are also membership sites and so are auction sites although there are no upfront fees for the latter.

A membership website provides you with a regular monthly income and they are incredibly easy to set up.

There are a number of secure software programs that can handle all your membership website requirements such as membership fees, login details, data management etc. Some are free but the paid ones are best and I recommend you go for one of these.

Here is the address of a website that has several good software programs...

https://colorlib.com/wp/software-for-creating-a-membership-site/

A membership website can grow exponentially as word gets around and others recommend it to their friends and family but if you take a proactive role in the site and make yourself personally available to your members it will grow much, much faster.

Don't confuse paid membership websites with forums, where everyone contributes for the good of all. And don't think that sharing a special interest is going to be enough to get people to part with their money.

The best membership sites are those that are exclusive to members only and offer real value that cannot easily be obtained elsewhere.

Although a membership website is not strictly a tangible 'product', you are still creating and offering a product, as much as a bank might offer you insurance.

Physical Products

The last type of product I'm going to cover in this chapter is probably the type many readers would have immediately thought this guide was purely about.

Yes, physical products that you create or make.

Now, obviously this can include an absolute multitude of items from window boxes to cakes and picture frames. If you can make it by hand in a garden shed or small workshop then it belongs here.

Working with wood is very popular and some people like to literally whittle away the hours making all manner of useful, everyday products. That's great... and to sell them you only need a website with photos of your products and then get to work marketing the website.

You can ether make, stock and sell or make to order. Making products to order is especially profitable and good for cash flow. Wedding cakes and special occasion bakery comes to mind. So does flower arrangements and tailoring.

In fact anything that there is a market for can be made if you have the necessary skills. To get an idea about what to make, visit a few craft fairs and note all the handmade goods. Craft fairs could also be an outlet for your own wares.

You are limited only by your imagination.

Photographs

There is an increasingly hungry market for unique photos and images, especially among web designers and online graphic professionals. If you have a quality camera and an interest in photography then you can make money from selling photos online.

Quality HD images are in demand and you can sell the same image over and over and receive continuous royalties for your efforts.

If photography is your thing and you like the idea of making regular money from it, and I don't mean anything to do with the 'Paparazzi', then get clicking.

First sign up to some of or all of the online stock photo websites. Here are links to some of the best:

http://www.shutterstock.com

https://stock.adobe.com

http://www.istockphoto.com

http://www.bigstockphoto.com

Plus there are many, many more... so do a search for stock photos and sign up for all of them.

Then take a look at the categories of photos, make a list then go out and do what you do best.

Upload your photos to all the websites and wait for the royalties to come in. You might only get 50 cents for each download but 50 cents x 200 a day is around £90. Okay it's not a fortune but it's regular and the more photos you can take and upload the more cash you can make.

There are hundreds of thousands of photos being sold every month, why not some of yours?

You need to get at least around 500 photos into the stock archives before you'll see any return but for every 1000 photos, you can increase your chances of success significantly.

If you manage to take any exceptional images you might try contacting subject related publications and offer them for a fair price. Sometimes it's a good idea to offer a freebie first by way of introduction and then offer them something that will really make them take notice.

Other branches of photography that can make more money is the age old wedding, christening, mother and baby, birthday photos, and any special occasion photos for that matter.

However, you will probably need a studio for most of that type of work and that means overheads. Fine if you have the clientele.

Music & Sound Effects

Royalty free music is needed now more than ever together with all manner of sound effects... why?

Video!

Online and offline video production often needs a soundtrack and in some cases sound effects too. If you take a look at some Youtube videos you will see virtually all of them will have a soundtrack. Now people will buy royalty free soundtracks just for this purpose, so if you play an instrument then you have a way of making some money by recording your tunes.

If you don't play an instrument, chances are you know someone who does and for a share of the fees you could ask them if you can record their jam sessions.

There's no need for vocals, just quality recordings of music covering all types of genres from classical to rock & roll. If you think of the music that accompanies some of the big blockbuster movies you'll get all sorts of great ideas for producing soundtracks.

In fact, just recently I was looking for a superhero type soundtrack for a video my team were producing. I searched all over the Internet and eventually found what I needed. I paid $35 for it and it's just 30 seconds long!

Sound effects are much easier to produce and anyone can do this. You just need to ensure the sound quality is good with no other sounds in the background.

To sell your recording you can either set up your own website or open an account with one of the royalty free stock websites and upload your recordings. Then wait for the commission payments to come rolling in.

Okay, so far we have covered some ways to create products both physical and digital, that you can sell but there's also a way you can make money by selling other people's products and services.

Strictly speaking this is not product creation but acting as a middle man or affiliate, for which you can make some very good money from commission payments.

I don't want to spend too much time on this subject as it a subject that will be covered in great detail in a later guide. However, it's worth a mention here because it offers an outlet and a way to sell your own products as well as selling other people's products.

Go to www.clickbank.com and check out the range of products being sold in the Marketplace. Then decide whether there might be an outlet for your own products or whether you could sell others for a big (75%) commission.

Then go over to www.jvzoo.com and do the same kind of research.

Another one to look at is www.click2sell.eu

CPA (cost per action) sites are another way to make money by promoting the product offers of others, only with many CPA offers you don't even have to sell anything. You can get paid just for sending leads to the offers. Take a look here. www.maxbounty.com

I'm sure you'll find something of interest amongst these websites.

Summary

Creating and selling your own product is probably the most satisfying way to make money. You become completely independent and you will have total control over the product and price.

However, before you get busy creating anything, do some research. Make sure there is a market for your products or you will just be wasting your valuable time and any financial investment.

Any and all of the product creation ideas mentioned in this guide will sell or make money. Some will sell offline, especially if they are physical products but try to think about online selling too because it's easier to reach your target market audience.

Digital products, especially information products, are best because there is an insatiable appetite for information and you can deliver them to the customer by digital download. No face to face selling, no shipping and handling costs and no duplication required.

Ebooks containing valuable information have accounted for many millionaires online, so make this idea one of your first to try.

Next we'll look at building websites. Now you don't have to be very tech savvy to build a website these days as there are plenty of easy DIY programs available.

However, it can help if you know the basics and that way there is less chance of you getting ripped off by some tongue twisting geeky web designer who is trying to blind you with science. (No offence to genuine web designers ☺)

Chapter 3

Introduction

Why would you want to know how to build your own website?

Okay, strictly speaking it's not necessary but if you know how a website should be properly constructed, then you have a big advantage over any of your competitors that don't.

Let's look at this way...

If you had a shop and you were selling a range of different products you could just put up shelves all over the place and then fill them with all manner of offerings.

However, if you arranged your shop in a way that made it easier for people to find the things they were looking for then you might give yourself a chance of selling more.

Some of the big clothes stores realised that if they had a large open space just inside the main entrance of the store then it made the store look more inviting and so more people ventured in.

Supermarkets have low shelving to ensure their customers can reach every item easily.

There is a reason why shops and stores are designed the way they are and it's no different for a website. The only difference is you have to design your website for both the customer and the search engines.

Being able to quickly build a website on demand will lift you out of the clutches of web designers and give you a very large degree of independence.

This has some obvious big advantages for you because you can quickly design and build a website in an hour or so instead of having to wait for your designer to get around to doing it for you, when it best suits him... or her.

This could take weeks!

You may never actually build a website yourself but if you know what should be done and what should go where and how to do it then you will always have the option of being in total control of your business.

That makes a lot of sense right?

Of course it does and that's why I've included a section on building your own website. I'll walk you through all the basics without getting too technical... promise!

Okay, let's do this...

Web Design Explained

There once a time when all web design work was hand coded using basic html language. HTML stands for Hyper Text Mark-up Language and was the standard code used for web page creation. This was a very long and tedious job and although other, more flexible types of codes began to get more favoured, the task was not made any easier until...

The WYSIWYG text editors arrived.

WYSIWYG stands for What You See Is What You Get and referred to a type of html editor that you could use in a design view as well as switching to a code view. This allowed you to quickly put together a website without having to have any knowledge of html code.

Two of the main WYSIWYG text editors were MS FrontPage and Adobe Dreamweaver. The former was discontinued by Microsoft but the latter has evolved with time and is used by many budding web designers.

As time passed many editors have become more sophisticated and now you can get free web page editors with many web hosting plans. I'll be looking at some of these as they offer a very quick and easy solution for some of the products you might be selling.

Other website editors started out as humble free blog software programs but have been high-jacked by web designers because they also offered the options to create web pages. The main and most popular of these programs is Wordpress.

Although Wordpress started life as a blogging platform, there are now millions of websites, which have been created from this free software. It has been developed through a collaboration of designers and coders, who all work to make it a unique and very flexible tool.

Wordpress keeps on growing as more and more developers add their expertise to the program and more and more add-ons, known as plugins are developed to work with the basic Wordpress installation.

One massive advantage about Wordpress is its ease of use, but it's also loved by Google because it ticks all the boxes in terms of design requirements.

Now, I don't want to lose you on this subject so I'm going to keep everything as simple as I possibly can... just like I promised.

You don't need to worry about coding and all that stuff but I will point out the important components of a website, so that you understand what makes a website work and what Google requires... or I should say demands of a website.

To keep everything simple I'm only going to be looking at Wordpress and one other free web design program, which comes free with a hosting account. Either of these will get you up and running from scratch and each will do their job but Wordpress will take you further.

There are quite a few hosting companies that now offer free websites and provide easy to use software, which allows you to construct a website in minutes. These basic websites are then hosted on their platforms.

What is hosting?

What is a platform?

If you're completely new to all this then some of the terms I talk about might sound like absolute jargon, so I'll explain as we go...

When you build a website it has to be hosted by a company that will allow the website to be accessible over the Internet. This is the hosting company and GoDaddy (www.godaddy.com) is a good example.

Most hosting companies also allow you to register a domain name, which is something else you will need to be able to get your website up and running.

In fact the whole process usually starts with a domain name registration so let's take a step back and look at this aspect in more detail.

A Step by Step Process

To help you better understand the process of getting a website onto the Internet, for example, let's say you want to start promoting DVDs (keeping it relevant).

So you decide on a domain name and you choose something like 'mediaproducts.co.uk' – the next thing you need to do is see if that domain is available. Go to www.godaddy.com or some other domain registration website like, www.lcn.com and do a check.

You'll have to come up with a list of relevant domains that suit your business because chances are many will have already been taken, especially the .com and .co.uk extensions.

So, let's assume a search reveals that your first choice domain name is not available, so you try for a variation like mymediaproducts.co.uk and a search shows that it is available. You may have to do this several times until you get domain names that suit your business and products

I would suggest you register 2 domains. One for the product and one for your business. By that I mean one domain containing the name of your product or type of product, if you can, and the other your business name.

Example: www.dvdmedia.co.uk – for your business products

Example: www.jpmpublishing.co.uk – for your business name

You only need one website but each domain can link to it

So, next you register your domains. Just go through the process of purchasing the domains for either 12 months or longer if you intend to keep them for any length of time.

Now that you have a domain you will need the domain to be hosted. Again you can do this with GoDaddy or any of the other domain registration companies, if they offer hosting packages. Whichever company you register your domains with, you might as well use their hosting services too.

I particularly like LCN.com because they offer easy web design, email, and a user-friendly control panel, which is all that's needed.

You just have to select the package you want from their many options. If using LCN, I suggest you go for the starter option, which is always the cheapest and will generally be okay to do what you need it to do.

If later you decide you need more hosting packages you can simply upgrade.

So now you have your domain and you have your hosting package. All you need now is your website.

Now, before we get into creating the website it's wise to have some idea about how you want the site to look. You'll certainly need some images and I recommend you buy these from a reputable image site.

Don't be tempted to just lift photos from the Internet because they will almost certainly belong to someone who will own all copyrights. If you do use images without permission or without paying it could cost you a lot of hard cash if you get caught... and you will. Getty Images will not hesitate to prosecute anyone who uses any of their images without paying for them, so you have been duly warned.

For a good selection of images just Google 'cheap royalty free images'.

Okay, so you have taken all the steps necessary to get to the point where you are now ready to build your website but if you want your website to be well received by Google, and the other search engines, then you need to bear in mind what these search engines are looking for in a website.

First a clean design is obvious, with nice quality images. Then you will need some web copy or web content as it sometimes called. This is basically some information about the products. For example if you are selling DVDs about Life Coaching you might write some content like this:

"Life coaching, or personal coaching as it is sometimes called, has its roots in executive coaching, which itself is derived from business management and leadership training.

It covers almost every aspect of personal development that you, as an individual might hope for and desire.

Although life coaching is associated with career development and management, executive and leadership skills, business start-up and entrepreneurialism, it also embraces personal fulfilment, life-balance, and the acquisition of specific skills, knowledge and experience

Setting yourself targets in order to reach goals requires a positive mental attitude combined with determination and a degree of self-discipline.

The benefits of goal-setting can be immense and it only takes a change of attitude to accomplish many wonderful things in your life.

Many highly successful people have achieved fame and wealth simply by taking control of their lives and focusing on personal goals.

This DVD set deals with all the necessary changes and adaptations needed to improve every area of your life.

Learn the techniques and strategies that have accounted for amazing success in both personal and business life.

There are now thousands of professional Life Coaches, which just goes to prove that there is a demand for this type of personal training.

And you might even consider becoming a highly paid life coach yourself.

To order a set of quality DVDs devoted to Life Coaching, simply **click here**"

That's about as much copy or content you need for each DVD product. The copy needs to be relevant and it needs to contain 'keywords'. Keywords are words that people might use when searching for this particular product. For example, 'life coaching', 'life coaching DVD' and 'life coaches' are all keywords or keyword phrases.

Keywords are an essential element of any website and I could write a whole book about them. (I probably will). However, suffice to say make sure you include the main keywords in your content but no more than 3 times for each keyword. Any more and the value of the keywords will become diluted.

If you want your site visitors to go to other pages on your website then make sure they can easily see the relevant links to those pages.

It's often a good idea to offer something for free to tempt your site visitors to buy. Something like a free ebook will often do the trick and you can find some very cheap ebooks with Private Label Rights or Resell rights by doing a search for 'cheap ebooks with resell rights'.

If you don't find anything suitable you can have an ebook written for you by an experienced copywriter. It only needs to be about 10 pages in length and should just cover basic stuff. Just as long as it has some perceived value.

Finally you need to show your site visitors what they need to do next to buy your product. This is the 'call to action'. It can simply be a 'Buy Now' button or a 'Buy Now' link. I'll cover the payment processing a bit later.

Design Your Website

So, everything is in place and you know how you want your website to look, so let's get on and build it...

Assuming you are going to use the LCN websites design tools, go to their design section... and simply follow the steps as outlined. It's all very straight-forward because these software programs have been designed for beginners.

You'll find similar easy to follow design programs with GoDaddy and many others including Hostgator, which are very cheap hosting service providers and worth checking out.

Hostgator have some design software options too like Weebly, which is a dream to use.

The Weebly web editor is so simple to use and incorporates a drag and drop system for images. It also has a readymade contact form and an image slider, which can add a real professional look to your website.

You'll also find other services on the control panel page including goMobi site Builder and some Wordpress tools...

Hostgator also offer an easy way to activate a Wordpress website from the hosting account right onto your domain name. You can just use their QuickInstall feature and a Wordpress site will be uploaded to your account.

Now, although I have mentioned GoDaddy and LCN in this guide, if I was to recommend a domain registration, hosting and free web design service provider then Hostgator would probably get my vote.

Their help and support service is very good too, which can save you hours of frustration should you become stuck on how to do something.

Well, you now have at your disposal several ways to get a website up and running, so in the next chapter we'll take a closer look at Wordpress.

Wordpress comes with free themes and paid themes. You have so many options with Wordpress especially when it comes to add-ons or plugins.

Wordpress For Websites

I mentioned earlier that Wordpress was originally intended to be a blogging software platform but is now considered to be a major player in website design.

Wordpress is free because it is not owned by any one individual or company. Instead it is what is known as Open Source, which means anyone can contribute to its evolution. It's written in a code called PHP and coders from all over the world contribute to it, making it better and more sophisticated.

It has grown over the years to become one of the most popular and important content management systems (CMS) in the world. There are currently around 75 million live websites, which have been built on the Wordpress platform.

With Wordpress comes many different themes, which you can customise with a few simple clicks. It also comes with a 'walk through' type of help feature, which any beginner would find invaluable.

I highly recommend Wordpress simply because it has just about everything you will ever need to be able to run an online business successfully. There are so many add-ons or plugins that you are literally spoilt for choice. A very large percentage of them are also free.

First, remember that a Wordpress site can usually be uploaded from any hosting package with just a couple of clicks. So assuming you have uploaded the platform to your hosting, here's a general explanation of what you'll see when you get inside.

When you login to your new Wordpress dashboard, you'll see instantly how easy everything is because you have a Get Started link and several other step-by-step links right in front of you.

On the left-hand side of your dashboard, you have several features including **Posts**, which is your blog, then **Media**, which is where you upload your images. Next is **Pages**, and this is where you create your web pages and add your content.

There's no need to bother with the **Comments** link or the **Marketplace** link at this stage. However, **Appearance** is where you can select your theme from the options or upload a new theme from the many hundreds of free themes available.

The **Plugins** link is where you can add and activate certain features like forms, backups, image sliders and just about anything you can imagine your website will ever need. The **Users** and **Tools** links are unlikely to be of any interest to you but the **Settings** link will.

Under this link you will find a sub-link for **General** settings and here you can input your site's title and tagline. When you click the Reading link you will see this page:

For your website to display online, make sure you select 'A static page' and your front page or home page and **Save Changes**. This is to ensure your website is live and not your blog posts, which you will not need.

For everything else use the **Help** link as the information is very clear. For further reading about Wordpress visit this link: http://www.wpbeginner.com/how-to-install-wordpress/

Payment Processing

So you have your website set up and you're ready to start selling your products, but how do you take payment?

There are a number of options but I always recommend **PayPal** because it's simple and easy, and we like simple and easy don't we?

If you don't already have a PayPal account then go here and open one right now: www.paypal.com

So what you need on your website to take payments from your customers is a Buy Now button. To create one you will need to create a Business Set-up or business account.

From your summary page click on the Tools link and scroll down to PayPal Business Set-up. Here you can select the option, by which you want to get paid, and for your website you will need to select 'On Your Website'.

Select the first option, *"Process all payments, including debit and credit cards, through PayPal."* Then click the Continue button.

Now select Option B and click on the 'Create payment button' link. Now all you have to do is complete the form and hey presto! Button code will be created, which can easily be inserted into your website page as text.

The PayPal button is instantly recognisable and a trusted online method for paying and receiving payments.

When a customer makes a purchase from your website, the money is collected for you and deposited into your PayPal account. PayPal charge a small transaction fee and the rest is yours to withdraw to your linked bank account.

It's the easiest and most convenient way of accepting online payments and I highly recommend you use this method.

You can also set up recurring payments and subscriptions with PayPal. If you also want to take card payments offline then PayPal offer the option to have a merchant account and will provide you with a (virtual) terminal.

There is a monthly fee for using this service but it is still a much cheaper option than using a merchant account through your High Street bank.

Checklist

You only have to decide whether you want to create a website using the free website builder provided by your domain registration and hosting company or go for a Wordpress website.

The former will not have as many features and the latter will allow you to add-on all manner of 'bells and whistles' to suit your business set-up.

Whichever way you choose to go remember to take a little time to think about how your website will look and what the search engines want from it in terms of content.

Look at any competitor or similar websites for inspiration and ideas. Take a look at some established websites that sell both single item products and multiples to get some ideas.

Choose a payment processing company like PayPal or if you don't like PayPal for any reason then go with www.2checkout.com - another simple system to set up on your site.

Now finally, once everything is set-up as you want it, register your website with the search engines. Just follow these links:

www.entireweb.com

www.freesubmission.com

www.isubmit.com

www.submitexpress.com

https://www.google.com/webmasters/tools/submit-url?hl=en_uk&pli=1

Next... you'll need to begin marketing and promoting your offers.

In this next section we'll look at the many options you have with both online and offline marketing.

Don't expect anyone to find your website unless you can point them in the general direction.

Chapter 4

Introduction

There are several ways to market your products online and during the course of running an online business you may have to try quite a few of them to determine which methods work best for you.

In this guide we'll look at all the methods, which can be considered mainstream, and I'm going to explain how to get the best from them.

More people are turning to the Internet to purchase products and services these days and so you have to find ways to advertise your products and get in front of the crowds. Successful Internet marketing is simply a numbers game. The more visitors you can get to your website or your ad or video then the more likely you are to makes sales.

Some of the most successful sellers on the Internet will use various advertising methods and test each one to see which one delivers the best return on investment (ROI). When they find the one method that works best they will plough tons of money into it until they have exhausted the market.

It's the way to make a quick killing but it takes a lot of cash and a lot of guts to be able to pull it off every time.

We'll be looking at a few less risky formulas and I'll also cover both paid and some free methods. Basically if you want to make money quickly it is going to cost you. If you don't mind waiting and are prepared to put in a little effort then the free method could prove to be the best method.

We'll start with Google Adwords, move onto Facebook ads and look at banner ads. Email marketing and article marketing deserves a mention also.

Google Adwords

This feature has been a massive money spinner for Google and that's because it works for them and it works for their customers too. When you search for something using Google you will see up to 4 ads on the top of the search results page and up to 4 at the bottom. These ads are triggered whenever a relevant subject is searched for with a keyword or keyword phrase.

The way Google Adwords works is you have to bid for those top positions. So each relevant keyword will have a price according to its popularity and you have to decide how much you want to bid. The highest bidders will get their ad into the highest position on the search page, and the ad will be triggered when a keyword that you are bidding on is used in a search.

So if we look at the search term 'used car dealers in chelsea', for example. This is a keyword phrase, which contains a number of keyword variations. For example you could have:

Used car dealers Chelsea

Used car dealer Chelsea

Chelsea used car dealers

Chelsea used car dealer

Car dealer Chelsea

Chelsea car dealer

And so it goes. Each phrase has a value attached to it but you can bet the best one, and the most expensive, would be 'used car dealers chelsea'. Certain words, especially conjunctions like 'and', 'if' and 'but' are discounted in keyword phrases, as are 'in' and 'of'.

So, getting your website, or in this case an ad, which contains a link to your website, into the top search results doesn't have to cost an arm and a leg in SEO fees. You can just create a Google Adwords ad and get there right away... at a price you can control. You only pay when someone clicks on your ad. That's why it's called pay-per-click (PPC)

Your ad can also be shown on a whole network of websites that contain content similar to that, which you are promoting. This is an option you can choose when setting up your ad campaign.

Another option is pay-per-view (PPV). With this option you pay a set amount for every 1000 views (impressions) your ad gets regardless of whether anyone clicks on the ad or not. It's best to try all options to see what works best for you.

To get involved with Google Adwords you must first open a Google Adwords account. You then need to fund your account with a budget to cover your advertising. Google gives you all the tools you need to create your ad and there's plenty of help and advice available too.

I recommend you have a good read through all their help pages first, so that you fully understand how PPC works. Make a special note to read about Quality Score in respect of your website's content, as this could save you a lot of money in the long run and get your ad shown more often.

Another aspect of successful Google Adwords advertising is understanding keywords and their relevance. It's not always obvious which are the best keywords for your products or services and so you might need to carry out a little keyword research. There are a number of online tools to help you with this aspect. Here are some website urls to a few...

http://keywordtool.io/

http://www.wordstream.com/keyword-tools

http://tools.seobook.com/keyword-tools/

You will also find Google's own keyword tool from within your Adwords account. It's also very useful but don't depend on it completely as sometimes the alternatives can throw up some real gems. https://adwords.google.co.uk/KeywordPlanner

Okay, so if you want to try Google Adwords, it certainly has many advantages but be prepared to get into a bidding war with your rivals.

You'll find plenty of help in getting started when you open an Adwords account.

Facebook Ads

Facebook advertising is in some ways very similar to Google Adwords except Facebook has a big advantage. People use it more often. In fact many people all over the world are using Facebook for communication purposes almost constantly. With over 1.4 billion people active on Facebook it's the place to go to sell your wares.

Facebook ads are shown all over the network and shown to audiences according to your demographic settings. You can therefore target a specific age group who have specific interests in specific subjects etc.

Facebook make it easy to get your ad right in front of the right people but unfortunately most of them are too busy chatting with their friends or posting selfies or sharing videos etc.

So unlike Google, Facebook ads are not always welcome and the problem with that is they can get ignored. Eventually people just get around them, avoid them and then the ad becomes powerless. Now I'm not saying you shouldn't at least try Facebook ads but don't expect results to be anything worth getting into a sweat about.

The trick with Facebook ads is to try to make the ad look less like an ad. If you can make it look like a story and include a great image then you're half way to getting your ad checked out, at least.

The majority of people using Facebook fall into the 'younger' category so this should be kept in mind if deciding to give it a go. However, with that in mind a product that has mass appeal to a younger audience might just sell very well.

To advertise on Facebook you obviously need an account. Then, when your account is open simply go to the Create Ads link on your Facebook page and get started.

Facebook make it easy for you to set up your ad campaign by prompting you to work on creating an objective. They will then guide you through the process of creating the right type of ad for your business.

By following their step-by-step ad creation formula you can really laser target your ad at very specific types of people. So, with all this working in your favour, it's certainly worth a try... for a short while at least.

Running a Facebook ad campaign is not the same as creating a Facebook page for your business and then putting your Facebook page link all over the Internet. However, there can be some confusion about the two when people talk about social marketing.

On the subject of social marketing, Twitter has advertising options too, although you can just send out short messages to anyone following you and include a link back to your website.

Instagram is another kind of social media platform based solely around sharing photos. However, you can also include a caption with your photos and that can include your website address.

The whole spectrum of social media marketing deserves much more time than can be afforded in this guide, so if this is an area of advertising that appeals to you then I suggest you carry out some research on each of the following.

Twitter.com

LinkedIn.com

Pinterest.com

Googleplus.com

Tumblr.com

Instagram.com

Reddit.com

Flickr.com

I have purposely left one very important social media name off this list and that's Youtube.

Youtube is an extremely powerful video sharing platform that can have truly amazing results for any marketing campaign, and that's the next subject we're going to be looking at now.

Youtube Video Marketing

I've included video marketing in this guide because it's a very important player in the world of online advertising and marketing. Video can work for you if it's sitting on your website or whether it's uploaded to Youtube and other video sharing platforms.

Video has a lot going for it because it can be all things. It can be informative, entertaining and engaging. Not only that! People just love video. They are sharing videos all over the world right now. Videos get hundreds of millions of views every day. It seems people just want to watch videos for all kinds of reasons.

Now, when you think about it... compare a text ad with a video ad.

In a text ad you try to explain the benefits of your product and hope someone will read about it. You can include a photo or a relevant still image. Whilst with a video ad you can demonstrate how a product works, add numerous images, smiling faces, and tell the viewer what to do next.

There's just no comparison. Video will always out-perform text ads, brochures and flyers every time.

One the most surprising things about video marketing is how cheap it can be. For example a full page advertisement in a magazine might cost over £1000, whilst a video, which says everything the text ad says and a lot more, can cost as little as £200.

I rest my case...

Now let's look at how best to use video to promote any type of product or service online and how to use other people's videos to gain visitors to your own website...

First, how do you get traffic to your website from your own video?

Youtube is the biggest and most popular of all the video sharing websites and it's owned by Google.

It doesn't cost anything for you to upload a video to Youtube. All you need is a channel and you can create one of those for free too. Just go over to **www.youtube.com** and open an account. If you haven't already, you might need to open a Google+ account, as Google likes to keep everything in one place.

So, once you have your channel all set up you just need to start uploading videos...

You can either create your own or get one of the many video production companies to create a video for you. To find one, just do a Google search for 'video production'.

Your video needs a few essential elements, the first one being a script. It's not necessary to have a storyboard type of script but it will need a voiceover script and that's because your video does need to have a recorded voiceover. A video without some verbal direction or explanation is like an old black and white silent movie... useless for advertising.

The voiceover script will also determine how the video is created, in terms of storyline, because the imagery will follow the script so everything makes sense.

Now, if you are making your own videos you can use a camcorder or you can just make life easy and use any of the free video maker software programs. Then buy some images relevant to your script and put together a series of photos to tell your story or promote your products.

Here's a couple of links to some examples:

https://www.youtube.com/watch?v=o1E921toaE0

https://www.youtube.com/watch?v=h6Z9ignsm4c

So, you've got the software, you've got the images, you've got the script and now you need the voiceover professionally recorded, and you need a backing soundtrack.

For the recording simply go to www.fiverr.com and search for 'voiceovers'. Here you'll find male and female professionals from the UK, US and many other countries. Just select one, pay a small fee and send them your script.

For backing tracks go to: www.jewelbeat.com and find something suitable for around $2.99.

So you now have all the components for making a great marketing video to promote your products. There's just one more thing...

When you upload your video to Youtube you need to carefully choose a title because in the tile you need to put your main keyword(s). Remember, keywords are vital for search and if you want your video to be found then this is a must do.

Next, always put a description... but you can simply use your voiceover script for this. At the very beginning of your description write Click Here: Followed by the full url of your website. For example:

Click Here: http://www.mywebsite.com

By writing the full url, which includes the **http://www** part you will make this link live and anyone going to watch your video can simply click on the link and hey presto! You have them on your website.

You can of course put your video on your website too by going to your channel, selecting the video and then clicking on the 'share' link below your video. This will then reveal some code, which you can copy and paste into your web page wherever you want the video to appear.

So you do this once and it will go on bringing visitors to your video and your website for months and even years to come.

Another way to get visitors to your website with videos is to select the videos option when you are setting up your Google Adwords. So instead of your ad showing up in the general Google search pages, it will be displayed at the bottom of any video that fits your keywords.

I'm not sure how successful this is because most people will close the ad before it has run because they just want to watch the video and an advertisement in front of it is a bit of a nuisance. However, there seems to be a lot of ads so someone must be making it work, and in that case it may be worth a try.

Now, although Youtube is the main video sharing website you can also put your video on others like www.dailymotion.com and www.metacafe.com plus many more.

Instead of spending a lot of time uploading your video to the many relevant sites, just go back to fiverr.com and search for 'video marketing'. You'll find a number of people who will put your video on 10 or 20 video sharing websites for just $5 and worth every cent.

Articles & Press Releases

There are other effective ways to market your products online and these involve a little writing on your part. If however, writing is not for you then you can outsource the writing to someone on fiverr.com.

The idea behind article marketing is that articles get read and people will link to the articles if they are looking for content for their websites. Also, if anyone wants to use your article they can, but it must remain intact including a backlink to your website in the short bio at the end of the article.

So the idea is to create an article, which is interesting and informative, and which people will enjoy reading. Your article can then go viral bringing valuable visitors to your website from the link at the end.

One of the main distributors of articles is www.ezinearticles.com - It's free to join and you can submit as many articles in as many categories as you want for free exposure and free traffic.

As I said earlier, you just get someone on fiverr.com to write the article for you but you must ensure the article is unique and not copied or 'spun' from some other article.

There was a time when article marketing was a major player in the world of Internet marketing until Google decided to change their algorithms concerning duplicate content. However, there is still some mileage in article marketing and is worth putting a few out there.

You can also put the same article on other article distribution sites like these:

www.articlecity.com

www.goarticles.com

Moving on...

Press releases are very under-rated but can bring huge results.

The idea behind a successful press release is obviously news. News is valuable and people want to know what's new and what's happening in all kinds of sectors, not just in business.

The great thing about press releases is the distribution company will have a network of news outlets and news sharing platforms together with links to publishers, publications, journalists and even some daily rag reporters.

If it's news worth reading, everyone is on it in a flash. Now, the best distribution companies are those who charge a fee for distribution services because they WILL put your release out into the public domain.

Like articles you can have a link back to your website, which will bring traffic but unlike an article it will not be a trickle... it is more likely to be a gush!

Writing press releases is a bit of an art and I would recommend you read some first before attempting to write one. Again, if writing is not your thing, turn to fiverr.com and you'll find someone more than capable of writing a release for you.

Once you have the press release written in the correct format, take a look at the distribution companies.

By far the most popular is PR Web (www.prweb.com). They offer various services all related to getting your release out to the masses.

It's free to open an account and they have a tariff of fees depending on the kind of distribution you need.

They can make your release circulate all over social media like Facebook and Twitter, getting readers from anywhere in the world. It really is a very powerful means of getting our message out there and it works.

Other PR distribution sites worth checking out include:

www.pressdispensary.co.uk

www.prmax.com.uk

www.releasewire.com

You can also submit your release to many free submission sites but the results will be less dramatic. However, still worth a try. Use fiverr.com to find someone to do a mass submission for you. It will be worth every penny.

Other Online Marketing

Blogs…

A Blog or WEB log is becoming a very popular way of getting subscribers, which you can convert to customers… over time. You have to be quite dedicated to writing blogs so I won't dwell too much on the subject here.

Perhaps it would be best for you to do your own research into blogs and determine whether you think you have the time to devote to creating and maintaining one.

Although we have now covered the main methods for advertising and marketing, there are certainly many more worth a brief mention in this guide.

SEO

The first one is SEO. This is Search Engine Optimisation and is concerned with getting your website ranked on the first page of Google's search results for your keywords. You will need to take a cautious approach here though because there are literally thousands of 'SEO Experts' who all promise they can get your site onto the first page.

The reality is, this is not something that can be done quickly and there is an ongoing cost. Basically, the more websites there are in your niche, the less likely yours will get on that front page.

Banner Ads

Banner ads are not as effective as they used to be but can still capture those inquisitive types, if the banner is unusual or eye-catching enough.

You can choose to have a banner ad set up in your Google Adwords account or use one of the independent banner ad distribution networks like:

www.buysellads.com

www.media.net

www.conversantmedia.com

www.adblade.com

Basically the price you pay for you banner advertising is based on per thousand views so could be worth a try as the cost is quite low. You can use fiverr.com to get a banner designed exactly how you want it. It will have a link back to your website bringing visitors with each click.

Advertorials

An advertorial is an advertisement disguised as an editorial feature. The idea is to write a report type feature, which is biased towards the product you want to promote. You then include a link back to your website at the end, indicating readers should click the link for more information.

Advertorials can work very well if you can get the piece into an online publication that your prospects are likely to read. Some E-zines (electronic magazines) and online 'newspapers' will publish your advertorial and prices vary considerably.

Email Marketing

Email marketing deserves the space of a whole guide to itself because to do email marketing the right way can be a little complex for the beginner. However, here's the basics...

The very best way to do this form of marketing is to install an email capture form on your website. However, prospects are not going to give you their name and email for nothing, so you need to tempt them by giving them something for free. In many cases this is usually an information guide or ebook, which they can download.

When a visitor types their name and email into the capture form and clicks on the 'Submit' button they are sent an email automatically from an autoresponder that has already been set up for this purpose. In the email they will have to confirm that they are asking for the free product or subscribing to your free newsletter by clicking on a link in the email.

When they do this they have effectively given you permission to email them and so you do... with your offers. The **list** you will be building this way is known as a 'warm' list as opposed to a 'cold' list. A cold list is a list of emails you might buy from a broker and the response rate from these will be very low, usually below 1% in many cases.

So, it's obviously best to generate your own lists, using free and valuable products. You can then nurture those lists and keep customers buying from you for life.

Affiliate Marketing

Affiliate marketing is where someone sells a product for you, and you then pay them a commission. This type of marketing can work for many different types of products, both tangible and virtual. If you checkout this website www.clickbank.com you'll see many different categories and many different products. These are vendors, who are using the Clickbank marketplace to recruit sellers for them, and they will pay those sellers very large commissions. In some cases as much as 80%.

The idea is you recruit a whole army of affiliates selling your products all over the Internet. This method has accounted for many Internet millionaires over the years as is still a very good way to sell your products. Other affiliate networks worth checking out are: www.jvzoo.com and www.click2sell.com

It doesn't cost you anything to join one of these networks except the commissions and network fees for taking part.

I hope I have given you some useful ideas for your own marketing.

I highly recommend you look at the products on offer in the Clickbank Marketplace and those on JV Zoo. Not only are there some good opportunities to make money from promoting these products for BIG commissions, you will get an avalanche of ideas too.

Summary

For this checklist I have put in order those methods, which I think you should try first when marketing your own products...

Google Adwords

Facebook Ads

Youtube (Video marketing)

Email Marketing (If you are experienced)

Press Releases

Article Marketing

Advertorials

Banner Ads

Note: There are several ways you can get free advertising. For example, by placing an ad on websites such as www.friday-ad.co.uk or www.craigslist.com and there are many others.

I don't actually recommend you use any of these for your advertising because there is little hope of selling anything and you'll get mountains of spam emails.

In the next and final section of this guide I want to look at advertising your business, products and services, offline.

Long before the Internet this was the only way to promote a product or service and there's still some mileage in this as you will see...

Chapter 5

Introduction

Long before the Internet, most advertising was restricted to newspapers, magazines, journals and newsletters. Printed ads and sales letters were the tools that made many millionaires back in the day before the Internet changed everything.

Now, although newspaper readership has declined drastically over the past few years, there has been an upsurge in specialised magazines, covering just about every topic of interest from baking to fishing.

There is also some evidence that sales letters still work, depending on the product being offered and to whom it is being offered.

In this chapter we'll look at ways you can use offline advertising to your advantage including using it as a funnel to get prospects to visit your website.

We'll look at newspaper ads and magazine ads and how best to word them, maximising impact within a very limited space. There is also a way to get your advertising for a much cheaper rate than the advertised rate card, and I'll explain how to do this.

Other methods include flyers, brochures, postcards and newsletter ads. We'll look at them all and then you can decide whether they could work for you.

The sales letter can work well if it is targeted at the right audience, so we'll need to look at mailing lists also. However, the long form sales letter of the 60s, 70s and

80s has since evolved. It is now less than half the length it used to be and for good reason.

Everyone is too busy...

We all seem to have very short attention spans these days and there's always something else that needs to be done or read... or whatever.

I don't want to sound like I'm 'waxing lyrical' but there once was a time when people looked forward to getting letters. They would put the kettle on, make a cuppa and sit down to read them religiously.

Not any more...

Print Ads – Newspapers

According to Press Mag Media, there are 13 million copies of newspapers sold every day, so someone is buying them. What this means is it's still a good way to advertise products but it's not a good way to try and sell those products directly.

There are stringent rules relating to selling products and services directly in newspaper ads, and you don't really want to become embroiled in all that because it can prove to be very costly. Instead we'll look at how to advertise much more effectively and for much less cost.

National newspapers or local newspapers?

Obviously national newspapers are going to want more of your ad spend than a local paper so you must determine whether the expense will bring a good return. Things to consider...

First, it's important to pitch your advertising at the right level, to the right type of person. You need to be communicating directly to the consumer who wants to buy your product. Consider age, gender, education, cultural background, and income of your prospect.

The higher the readership, the more chance you'll enjoy a good response. So, although an ad in a national paper might cost more it could potentially yield more. When checking readership figures quoted, make sure they are from the National Readership Survey, which is the gold standard for the media industry.

Repetition of small ads is key, especially if they are getting at least a break-even response. Nine out of ten buyers continue to look at the vendor's adverts after making a purchase. Continual advertising reassures buyers that they have made a good decision.

In the case of small ads, frequency is vital, with weekly insertions being recommended. Three to four adverts should yield a steady response that builds with each insertion. The longer the series the less risk you take and the greater the chances your campaign will work.

Focus your advertising on your products and the benefits to the consumer. Don't worry about promoting your brand, as that can have an adverse effect on business finances, unless you have a very large budget of course.

So, if you decide to advertise your products in the national press you need quite a large budget but there is the possibility it could pay off. However, if just starting out you might want to leave that until you have a few sales under your belt.

Instead, and to test the water, so to speak, you could try local advertising... and what better than a cheap ad in a free newspaper?

If free papers are delivered in your area, then look at the ads. They can be much larger than those in national papers because they cost so much less. And people do read these papers so it's a good place to start a test ad.

Depending on your budget you could just skip this trial and go directly for the local or regional paper. It will cost more than the free paper but will most definitely have a larger readership.

So, assuming you are going to try the local paper, what should you put in your ad?

It all starts with a headline...

I'll make several references to the headline throughout this guide because it is just so important.

Here is an example of how a small classified ad for promoting a DVD, in a local newspaper, should be laid out.

Cleanse Your Body & Mind - Learn Yoga

Learn Yoga in the comfort of your own home. New DVD reveals the mysteries and the benefits of this ancient technique.

Visit: www.yogaforyou.co.uk

The headline should state a main benefit and attract attention.

The body copy should give some details, features or more benefits.

Then there is the call to action. In this case it's "visit the website".

So what this ad is doing is generating leads for your website, where you have the product image and a lot more information. Plus you are able to take payment from your website, which makes everything very convenient.

Another possible call to action would be to call a telephone number, which would be the number of the fulfilment company, who will then take credit card payment details over the phone and despatch the order for you. You can find a number of fulfilment companies on the Internet by 'Googling' the phrase 'fulfilment company'.

So advertising in newspapers should be used to generate leads. This is a much cheaper option than trying to sell the product right off the page. And as mentioned already, you would be limited in your ability to do this because you have to be a member of MOPS. This is the Mail Order Protection Scheme.

Don't go there!

Instead, focus solely on using newspaper ads to get people to your website, where all the action can take place.

Advertorials

Whilst still on the subject of newspaper advertising I should just mention advertorials.

Ad advertorial is basically an ad in editorial form. It is designed to go into a newspaper, look like news and read like news but is really promoting a product or service.

If you're the creative type you might want to try writing an interesting 'story', heavily biased in favour of your product.

Sometimes local papers run features and will print a well-written story about the topic of the week, month etc. for free.

So, is advertising in newspapers the way to go for you?

That is for you to determine, but it's a consideration that may be worthy of the time and money, although there are other alternatives to consider also.

Small classified ads, under section headings such as Health, Sport or Special Interests may be useful. If others are already advertising products similar to the ones you are promoting then it might be worth a try.

Here's a tip for saving money on advertising in newspapers...

Find out when the publication deadline is for ads similar to something you would like to place. Then phone the newspaper on that day and ask them to give you their best price for inserting your ad.

Hold out until the deadline and you will very likely be offered a special 'distress rate'.

This is where the paper has space to fill and will offer very low rates just to do it. That's where you can save a bundle of cash on your advertising.

It works with classifieds, features and advertorials.

Print Ads – Magazines

Advertising in magazines is probably a much better bet than newspapers for products such as books and DVDs. Also, you can very often get the ads a bit cheaper than if placed in newspapers. A full colour ad in a glossy mag is worth its weight in gold, especially if it's the right magazine.

By that I mean, if it's likely to have a readership that matches your criteria, in respect of demographics.

For example, a woman's magazine (and there are plenty of them) would be the ideal medium for placing an ad about manicures and pedicures, or dressmaking or makeup related subjects.

There are so many lifestyle magazines around that there is bound to be at least one that will fit the bill regardless of whatever product you want to sell.

I suggest you go to your nearest WH Smith store and take a note of the magazine titles on the shelves and match them to the products you want to promote.

Writing ads for magazines is the same as for newspapers, with the headline and body copy plus a call to action. Take a look at existing ads in these magazines to get an idea about how to set them out. As for cost, work on the same principal as the distress rate tip I mentioned earlier.

The more magazines there are covering one subject or interest then the more likely there will be some good rates for your ads.

Some of these magazines also invite readers to send in their stories. That should give you some idea about the kind of reader these mags attract.

If you see the same ad or an ad for the same product in several different magazines, that's a sure sign those products are selling well.

Again, as with newspaper ads you can place small ads as lead generators or because a magazine lends itself better to a full glossy ad, and if your budget allows... why not go for it?

Brochures, Leaflets & Flyers

What is the difference between these three marketing items?

Brochures

When we think of brochures, we might think of about glossy holiday brochures or those home improvement handouts. Basically a brochure can be created for any type of business and is almost always glossy.

The brochure stands out amongst marketing pieces because it is representative of the company and not just their products and services. So it is also a means to increase brand awareness.

Brochures are not designed for reading and then disposing of. They have a life span. They can stick around for many years and are meant to be reference material. That's why so much goes into designing and developing them and not to mention the huge printing costs involved.

In some cases, brochures can resemble catalogues with pages and pages of products. However, where they differ from catalogues is that they carry more information about the company's products or services.

You would expect to see lots of images in a brochure, all tastefully photographed or photo-shopped and you might find a few short articles also.

In some brochures you will not find any reference to prices. This is especially true of any upmarket type publication as blatant price tagging would be far too vulgar.

Yet in others there will be prices falling off every page. This is the crude brochure and will generally be the cheaper version.

Leaflets

A leaflet comes somewhere between a flyer and a brochure.

It's basically a one-page A4 or A3 size sheet with one or two folds. The purpose of a leaflet is to provide just enough information via text and imagery in order to promote a product or service.

In general, leaflets are glossy and the graphics are well designed with the intention of having a large print run for mass distribution either by hand or by mail. They are particularly good at promoting special offers and sales but they will generally have a short life span so they have to create an immediate impact.

Many people will receive leaflets through their letterbox along with perhaps a newspaper or magazine. Also, your local takeaway will hand deliver them to you, usually adorned with images of scrumptious food to tantalise the taste buds.

Flyers

Some people have their own take on what a flyer is and some will say it's the same as a leaflet. My view is that a flyer is a one-page cheap and cheerful ad that is used mainly to promote an event or offer.

For example, a flyer might be created to promote a local fete or school open day, a bingo hall or a night club. Generally a flyer will have poor graphics and border on an amateurish print job.

They are generally handed out in public places or posted door to door. In contrast a leaflet is usually better designed and contains much more information. A flyer is usually a full A4 or A3 size piece of cheap and sometimes coloured paper.

That's the difference between them in both design and print.

Flyers are quite useful for promoting a business's special offers and products but obviously has a very short life span, with many destined for the nearest bin. And it's because of this short life span that it really does need to create a big impact right away.

An example might be a fruit and veg shop, which has to clear its surplus fruit very quickly, so the flyer might be worded something like, "Special Offer Today Only - Bananas Only 10p A Pound!"

So that's the main differences...

As far as advertising your products is concerned, they can all play a part.

However, the brochure would most probably be the best choice and most suitable. Brochures can be mailed out to a list or you can leave them in places like gyms, leisure centres and health spas, with the managers' permission of course.

Printing can be quite inexpensive these days because there is a lot of competition for your custom. Check out www.vistaprint.com who offer exceptional deals and will print small quantities too.

In most cases you can design your brochure on their website, which saves a lot of time and money.

The Sales Letter

There once was a time when millions of pounds could be made by using a simple sales letter to sell your products. However, with the Internet now becoming the mainstream tool of marketers and the ever-increasing costs of postage, the sales letter has almost slipped into oblivion.

Well, not quite...

People still like to receive mail and so there is still a chance that the sales letter can work for you. Copywriters often tell us that the more you tell, the more you sell. Could this be a ploy to get their clients to part with more money for really long letters?

No!

It's actually true, or at least to some degree. If you are trying to persuade a reader of your sales letter to spend a lot of money with you then you have to justify that sale, and that means lots of sales copy.

Alas! People seem to have less time and patience to sit down and read a 24 page sales letter these days and so the letter has to get to the point faster and provide some evidence or credibility much sooner.

A 6-10 page letter is more the norm these days but better still is the one-page intro letter displaying a link to a website.

Now, I think both work as well, and so it might be worth trying both. First though... how do you find names and addresses to send to?

Well, just go to a list broker, who for a fee, will provide you with a list of names that fit your criteria. For example go to: www.listbroker.com

Here you'll find mailing lists of mail order buyers that you can rent and send out your sales letters to.

Another list broker worth checking out is: www.hilitedms.co.uk

List prices vary depending on the size of the list and the value of the list, in terms of the average spend of the list names.

One thing I should mention here is that there are lots of list brokers but basically you get what you pay for.

By that I mean if you are prepared to pay the right price you will get a good clean list, that has been updated regularly and therefore there is much more chance your letter will get to the person on the list.

If you go for a much cheaper list from a dodgy broker, the list could be years old and many of the people might have moved away or be not at all interested in your product offer.

The Hilite list broker has been around for a long time and is tried, tested and trusted amongst many mail order gurus. Okay, so that's how you get a list of prospects to mail to.

The next part of the process is to get your sales letter written. If this is something you cannot do yourself then you will have to hire a copywriter. Select one that has experience in writing for direct mail and I would recommend you do NOT look on websites like www.freelancer.com to find one.

www.upwork.com might be okay, but you'll find better a quality writer on www.pph.com or just do a search for 'direct response copywriter'.

Copywriters' fees vary and so you might have to go through a selection process. Always ask to see examples of previous work. A copywriter that is well established is probably going to be the best choice. Ensure the copywriter can add images to the sales letter and design an order form.

Now, I mentioned earlier that an option is to send out a one-page sales letter in place of a 10 pager. The idea of a one page letter is to introduce the offer and then include the website address for the reader to go and visit for more information.

If you already have a website set up with sales letter and payment processing then it makes a lot of sense to send leads to it rather than try to convert them with a long letter.

But it might be worth trying both.

The one-page letter however has to do quite a big job in convincing the recipient to get of their backside, switch on their computer and check out your website. So it has to be convincing and enticing, create curiosity or offer the reader some kind of reward for taking the trouble.

You need a good headline, some interesting body copy and the address of your website, in BIG letters. Many marketers both new and professional use this approach to generating leads from their mailing lists.

Now, as I said earlier, people still like to receive letters, so there's no reason why this method should not work for you. However...

There is something else people like to receive in the mail, which can also get them excited, and that's a postcard...

Postcard Marketing

Postcard marketing has proved to be very successful in getting people to respond to the sales message, which is usually something like, "Visit our website now for more information".

The great thing about postcards is they are relatively cheap to produce. You can design your own on a website like www.vistprint.com for an absolute pittance. Let your imagination run away with you...

For example, if the front of your postcard depicts a scene of sand and sea with a healthy looking person just wandering along, then it will immediately look like someone you know has sent you a holiday postcard.

So, the recipient has to just turn it over to see who it's from and voila! Your message gets read. It's almost fool proof because everyone reads postcards.

I would highly recommend this method of offline marketing whatever product you are selling.

Summary

Print ads may be worth a try but in the great scheme of things, and especially if you are just starting out, I would say try the postcard method first. The exception is if you have a large budget, in which case newspaper and magazine advertising might see a good return.

Remember to leave placing your ad till as late as possible or as near to the publication deadline so that you can get distress rates for your insertion.

Brochures are a good idea because you can either send them out to a list or leave them at establishments that provide services related to your products. For example, gyms, spas and sports centres. You can design your brochure online using the facilities provided by Vista Print, and the cost is very reasonable.

Sales letters will work for certain products but if you decide to try this method then opt for the one-page sales letter or the intro letter first. See how this goes in terms of response and then go for the long form sales letter if it looks like it might work.

Postcards are one of the most convenient methods to use for offline marketing and I recommend you try using them because I know they can work well. Again Vista Print can provide the necessary design software for you and prices are really inexpensive.

About The Author

Bill Knight is a Direct Response Copywriter with over 30 years' experience in writing all manner of sales and marketing copy. He has worked with many successful Internet marketers and offline entrepreneurs over the years and knows what works best online and offline, in terms of product and service marketing.

He has also helped many start-up companies and individuals with essential elements of their businesses including web design, graphic design, copywriting and marketing for their products and services.

Bill is the founder of the successful UK businesses, Anglox Publications, Anglox Web & Graphic Design and BusyVids

He has personally been involved with multiple affiliate programs and CPA programs, Google Adwords and Facebook ad creation. Two of his specialities are Direct Response sales letters and email marketing.

He is a content marketing consultant and offers his services to clients throughout the UK.

Being an online entrepreneur himself he has vast knowledge and experience of a wide range of online promotions for numerous products and services. He is co-owner of the highly successful video production company, BusyVids.

He has a broad base of clients all over the world and they vary in experience from absolute beginners to highly successful multi-millionaire professionals.

You can learn more about Bill Knight here:

www.topcopywriter.co.uk & **www.busyvids.com**